A SUCCESSFUL JOB INTERVIEW

Sylvain MILON

CONTENTS

INTRODUCTION

Welcome to Successful Job Interviewing! This book has been specially designed to help you successfully navigate the job selection process and ace your job interviews. Whether you're a recent graduate looking for your first job, or an experienced professional looking for a new opportunity, the tips and strategies presented in this book will help you stand out from the crowd and land the job of your dreams.

In a competitive job market, it's essential to be properly prepared for a job interview. Preparation is the key to success, and this book will guide you through every step of the process. We'll start with the importance of preparation and give you practical advice on building a powerful CV and writing a convincing cover letter.

We'll then take you through the various stages of a job interview, explaining how to understand the selection process, how to answer frequently asked questions and how to master behavioral interview techniques. You'll also learn how to manage stress and anxiety during the interview, as well as the importance of body language and effective communication.

We'll give you practical tips on salary negotiation and benefits, as well as advice on how to avoid common mistakes that could cost you a job opportunity. In addition, we'll show you how to stand out from other candidates and use social networks strategically in your job search.

Finally, we'll look at telephone and online interviews, which are becoming increasingly common these days. You'll discover the best practices for succeeding in these types of interviews, and how to follow up professionally after the interview to maximize your chances of landing the job.

CHAPTER 1: THE IMPORTANCE OF PREPARATION

Preparation is one of the keys to a successful job interview. Many candidates underestimate its importance, thinking they can rely on their skills and experience to shine in the interview. However, proper preparation is what distinguishes average candidates from exceptional ones.

First of all, preparation allows you to better understand the company and the position for which you are applying. Thoroughly research the company, its industry, corporate culture and values. Find out about the company's recent projects, customers and competitors. This in-depth knowledge will help you formulate relevant answers during the interview and demonstrate your interest in the company.

Next, preparation allows you to familiarize yourself with the skills and qualifications required for the position. Carefully analyze the job advertisement and identify the key skills the employer is looking for. Next, review your own experience and skills, and prepare concrete examples of situations in which you have demonstrated these skills. This will enable you to answer questions about your qualifications accurately, and convince the employer that you are the ideal candidate for the job.

Preparation also includes preparing answers to questions commonly asked at job interviews. There are some frequently asked questions, such as "Tell me about yourself", "What are your strengths and weaknesses?", "Why do you want to work for our company?". Think about these questions in advance and prepare clear, concise answers. By practicing how to formulate them, you'll feel more at ease during the interview, and avoid scrambled or incoherent answers.

Another important aspect of preparation is interview practice. Practice answering questions with a friend or family member. Do mock interviews to familiarize yourself with the process and to get used to talking about your achievements and skills. Ask your interview partner to give you constructive feedback on your body language, tone of voice and ability to convey your ideas clearly and convincingly.

Finally, don't forget to prepare your questions for the employer. At the end of the interview, it's common for the employer to ask if you have any questions. This is an opportunity for you to show your interest and curiosity about the company and the position. Prepare a few pertinent questions about the company, the department in which you'll be working, growth opportunities, etc. In conclusion, preparation is the key to a successful job interview.

It allows you to better understand the company, familiarize yourself with the skills required, prepare your answers and practice in advance. By investing time and energy in your preparation, you greatly increase your chances of landing the job. Remember, thorough preparation is the first step to professional success.

Whether you're a beginner or a seasoned professional, "Réussir son entretien d'embauche" will give you the tools to

CHAPTER 2: UNDERSTANDING THE SELECTION PROCESS

The selection process during a job interview can vary from company to company, but there are generally common steps that most employers follow. Understanding this selection process will enable you to prepare better and approach each stage with confidence. In this chapter, we'll look at the different stages of the selection process and give you tips on how to succeed at each stage.

1. Screening: In many companies, the first step in the selection process is to screen applications. Employers examine CVs and cover letters to identify the most suitable candidates. To get through this stage, make sure your CV is clear, concise and relevant to the position. Highlight your most relevant experience and skills to attract recruiters' attention.

2. The first interview: Once you've been shortlisted, you'll usually be invited to an initial interview. This may be a telephone interview, an in-person interview or an online interview. The aim of this stage is to get to know you better as a candidate. Prepare yourself by answering frequently asked questions, demonstrating your motivation and professionalism. Be prepared to explain your

career path and highlight your past achievements.

3. Assessments: Some employers use assessments to evaluate candidates' skills. These may include personality tests, technical skills tests, situational exercises or case studies. Find out in advance what types of assessments the company uses, and prepare accordingly. Practice the tests and familiarize yourself with the skills and knowledge being assessed.

4. Subsequent interviews: If you pass the first interview, you may be invited to take part in further interviews. These interviews may involve human resources managers, team managers or company executives. Each interview will have its own objectives, so it's important to understand the role of each person you meet and adapt your pitch accordingly. Show your interest in the company, ask relevant questions and demonstrate how you can contribute to their success.

5. Reference checks: Before making a final decision, employers can conduct reference checks. Make sure you have professional references ready to share. Contact former employers or colleagues to get their approval, and let them know about the positions you've applied for. Be sure to provide references that can attest to your experience and skills relevant to the position.

6. The job offer: If you have successfully completed all the previous steps, you may receive a job offer. Take the time to evaluate the offer and negotiate the terms if necessary. Make sure you understand the job responsibilities, compensation, benefits and working conditions before accepting.

Understanding the selection process is essential to preparing yourself properly and maximizing your chances of success. By familiarizing yourself with each stage and preparing accordingly, you'll be able to demonstrate your value and convince employers that you're the ideal candidate for the job. Remember, every step is an opportunity to shine and show what you can bring to the company.

CHAPTER 3: BUILDING A POWERFUL CV

The CV is one of the key elements of your application and plays a decisive role in the selection process. A well-constructed, striking CV can help you stand out from the crowd of applicants. In this chapter, we'll explore the essential elements of a successful CV and give you tips on how to build a CV that will catch the attention of recruiters.

1. Clear, professional format: Choose a clear, professional format for your CV. Use headings, distinct sections and a balanced layout. Make sure the information is well organized and easy to read. Use a professional font and make sure the font size is appropriate.

2. Personal information: Start your CV by including your personal information. This includes your full name, address, telephone number and e-mail address. Make sure this information is up-to-date and professional.

3. Professional objective: Depending on your personal information, you can include a professional objective. This objective should be concise and specific. It should demonstrate your interest in the position and highlight your main skills and career objectives.

4. Professional experience: The professional experience section is one of the most important parts of your CV. Start with your most recent experience and work backwards. Include the name of the company, your dates of employment, your job title and a description of your key responsibilities and achievements. Focus on the results you've achieved and the skills you've developed.

5. Academic training: After the professional experience section, include a section on your academic training. Mention the degrees you've earned, the institutions you've attended and the years you earned them. If you have any relevant academic distinctions, don't hesitate to include them.

6. Skills: A skills section is essential to highlight your strengths and qualifications. Divide this section into technical skills and cross-cutting skills. Include specific skills related to the position for which you are applying, as well as general skills such as problem-solving, time management and communication.

7. Achievements and projects: If you have any noteworthy achievements or projects, don't forget to include them in a dedicated section. These could be professional achievements, academic projects or significant contributions in relevant fields.

8. Languages and computer skills: If you speak several languages or have specific computer skills, be sure to mention them in your CV. This can be an important asset, especially if the language or IT skills are relevant to the job.

9. References: Finally, you can include a section on references. Indicate that references are available upon request. Make sure you have solid professional references ready to share if needed.

When building your CV, remember to tailor each one to the position and company you're applying to. Tailor your content and skills to meet the specific needs of each employer. Proofread your CV carefully to eliminate spelling and grammatical errors, and make sure it is clear and concise.

A strong CV is a valuable asset in your job search. By building a well-structured CV and highlighting your relevant experience and skills, you increase your chances of attracting the attention of recruiters and landing an interview.

CHAPTER 4: WRITING A CONVINCING COVER LETTER

The cover letter is an essential part of your application. It's your chance to convince recruiters that you're the ideal candidate for the job. In this chapter, we'll explore the key elements of a convincing cover letter and give you tips on how to write a letter that will catch employers' attention.

1. Professional header: Start your cover letter with a professional header. Include your name, address, telephone number and e-mail address. Align this information on the right-hand side of the page.

2. Addressee and date: Under your heading, indicate the company name, the name of the recruiter or human resources manager, and the company address. Just below, indicate the date on which you are writing the letter.

3. Appropriate salutation: Use an appropriate salutation, such as "Dear Madam" or "Dear Sir", followed by the name of the recruiter or human resources manager. If you don't know the name of the recipient, you can use "Dear Recruiter" or "Dear Human Resources Manager".

4. Powerful introduction: Start your cover letter with a punchy introduction that grabs the reader's attention. Express your interest in the position and the company right from the start. You can start with a catchphrase, an anecdote or a relevant quote.

5. Highlighting your skills and experience: In the body of your letter, highlight your skills and experience that are relevant to the position you are applying for. Relate your qualifications to the requirements of the position. Use concrete examples to illustrate your past achievements and the skills you can bring to the company.

6. Personalization: Customize your cover letter for each company. Research the company and identify its needs, values and objectives. Use this information to show how you can contribute to achieving these goals and fit into the company's culture.

7. Motivation and interest: Show your motivation and interest in the position and the company. Explain why you are enthusiastic about working for this specific company and how you can contribute to its success. Show passion and determination in your letter.

8. Clarity and conciseness: Write your letter clearly and concisely. Avoid long sentences and dense paragraphs. Use simple sentences and avoid technical jargon. Make sure your ideas are well-organized and easy to follow.

9. Impactful conclusion : End your cover letter with an impactful conclusion. Reiterate your interest in the position and your availability for an interview. Thank the recipient for taking the time to read your letter, and include your contact details for a

possible follow-up.

10. Signature: End your cover letter with a polite phrase such as "Yours sincerely". Include your name and handwritten signature.

When writing your cover letter, remember to proofread carefully to eliminate spelling and grammatical errors. Also make sure that the letter is well formatted and corresponds to professional expectations.

A convincing cover letter can make all the difference in the selection process. By highlighting your skills, motivation and interest in the company, you increase your chances of attracting the attention of recruiters and securing an interview.

CHAPTER 5: PREPARING FOR FREQUENTLY ASKED QUESTIONS

During a job interview, recruiters frequently ask questions to assess your skills, experience and suitability for the position. Preparing for these questions is essential if you are to answer them clearly, concisely and convincingly. In this chapter, we'll look at some of the most common questions asked at job interviews and give you tips on how to prepare to answer them effectively.

1. Tell me about yourself: This question is often asked to give you the opportunity to briefly introduce yourself. Prepare a concise answer that highlights your qualifications, experience and career goals. Focus on the elements most relevant to the position you're applying for.

2. Why do you want to work for our company? This question is designed to assess your interest in and knowledge of the company. Research the company thoroughly before the interview and identify its values, culture and achievements. Highlight the

aspects that appeal to you and explain how your profile matches what the company is looking for.

3. What are your strengths and weaknesses? When you talk about your strengths, highlight your key skills and past achievements. Be specific and give concrete examples to illustrate your points. As for your weaknesses, identify one or two that are not critical to the position, and explain the steps you are taking to improve them.

4. Where do you see yourself in five years? This question assesses your long-term vision and professional ambition. Be realistic in your answers and highlight your desire to progress and take on new challenges. Avoid answers that are too generic, and try to link your vision to the company and position for which you are applying.

5. How do you handle stress and difficult situations? Employers are looking for candidates who can deal with stress and difficulties calmly and effectively. Prepare concrete examples of stressful situations you've encountered in the past and explain how you managed them. Highlight your time management, problem-solving and communication skills.

6. Tell me about a project or achievement you're proud of: Select an achievement or project relevant to the position and explain the details. Focus on the challenges you faced, the steps you took to overcome them and the results you achieved. Show how this experience demonstrates your ability to achieve objectives and bring value to the company.

7. How do you work in a team? This question is designed to assess your ability to collaborate with others. Prepare examples of projects or situations where you have worked effectively as part

of a team. Highlight your communication skills, your ability to listen to others, your flexibility and your commitment to common goals.

8. Why did you leave your last job? If you left a previous job, be honest and positive in your answer. Avoid criticizing your former employer, and focus on the professional reasons that led you to seek new opportunities. Focus on what you learned from the experience and the skills you acquired.

9. Do you have any questions for us? At the end of the interview, you'll usually be given the opportunity to ask your own questions. Prepare a list of relevant questions about the company, the position, the corporate culture or development opportunities. This will demonstrate your interest in the company and your desire to learn more.

When preparing to answer these questions, take time to think about your answers and practice them out loud. Be sure to answer clearly and concisely, using concrete examples to illustrate your points. Keep in mind that the objective is to show how your skills, experience and personality match the needs of the company and the position.

CHAPTER 6: DEVELOPING GOOD COMMUNICATION SKILLS

Communication skills are essential in all aspects of professional life, including job interviews. Good communication enables you to express your ideas clearly, connect with others and convey your message effectively. In this chapter, we'll explore the importance of communication skills in job interviews and give you tips on how to develop them.

1. Active listening: Good communication starts with active listening. When you're in an interview, listen carefully to the questions you're asked and make sure you understand what's being asked. Take time to think before you answer, and be open to comments and suggestions. By listening carefully, you'll be able to formulate relevant and appropriate responses.

2. Clarity and conciseness: When answering questions, be clear and concise. Avoid long, complex sentences that could confuse your message. Use simple, direct language to convey your ideas effectively. Organize your ideas logically and use concrete

examples to illustrate your points.

3. Non-verbal language: Non-verbal language plays an important role in communication. Pay attention to your body language, posture and facial expressions during the interview. Maintain eye contact with recruiters and show commitment and interest in your interactions. Positive non-verbal communication reinforces your message and conveys your confidence and professionalism.

4. Adaptability: The ability to adapt to different interlocutors is crucial in communications. Every recruiter may have a different communication style, so it's important to adjust accordingly. Adapt your tone, language and level of detail to suit the person you're talking to. Pay attention to non-verbal cues and adjust your communication accordingly.

5. Conflict management: Conflict management is an integral part of communication skills. If you are confronted with a difficult question or delicate situation during an interview, keep calm and remain professional. Listen carefully to other people's points of view, express yourself respectfully and seek constructive solutions. The ability to handle conflict effectively demonstrates your maturity and aptitude for teamwork.

6. Communication practice: To develop your communication skills, practice regularly. Engage in conversations, debates or presentations. Do improvisation exercises to improve your responsiveness and adaptability. Use online resources to practice answering interview questions. The more you practice, the more you'll gain in confidence and communication skills.

7. Feedback and improvement: Ask for feedback after the interview to find out your communication strengths and areas for

improvement. Use this feedback to continually improve and refine your communication style. Be open to advice and suggestions, and use them to develop yourself professionally.

By developing good communication skills, you'll be able to convey your message clearly, connect with recruiters and create a positive impression at job interviews. Practice regularly, pay attention to non-verbal cues and adapt your communication to suit your interviewer. Effective communication is an invaluable asset for your professional success.

CHAPTER 7:
MANAGING
INTERVIEW STRESS
AND ANXIETY

Job interviews can be stressful and anxiety-provoking situations for many candidates. Stress and anxiety can be detrimental to your performance and your ability to convey your best side to recruiters. In this chapter, we'll look at the importance of managing stress and anxiety during the interview and give you tips on how to overcome them.

1. Understand your stress: The first step to managing stress and anxiety during an interview is to understand the sources of your stress. Identify the negative thoughts, apprehensions and fears that contribute to your anxiety. For example, you might fear not answering questions correctly, not living up to expectations or being judged by recruiters. By identifying these sources of stress, you can manage them better.

2. Prepare properly: Thorough preparation is essential to reduce interview stress. The better prepared you are, the more confident you'll be in your answers. Research the company, the position and

common interview questions. Practice answering these questions and prepare concrete examples to illustrate your skills and achievements. The better prepared you feel, the less stress you'll experience.

3. Use relaxation techniques: Before the interview, use relaxation techniques to calm your mind and body. Deep breathing, meditation, positive visualization or exercise can help reduce stress and anxiety. Take a few minutes to relax and refocus before the interview. This will help you approach the interview in a calmer, more relaxed frame of mind.

4. Adopt a positive mindset: Cultivate a positive mindset before and during the interview. Replace negative thoughts with positive affirmations. Remind yourself of your strengths, skills and past achievements. Visualize yourself succeeding in the interview and confidently answering the questions asked. A positive mindset will help you stay motivated and overcome stress.

5. Be aware of your body language: Your body language can influence your stress level. Pay attention to your posture, breathing and facial expression during the interview. Keep your posture upright, breathe deeply to relax and smile naturally. Confident body language sends positive signals to recruiters and helps you feel more at ease.

6. Stay focused on the present: Anxiety can often be fuelled by thoughts about the future. During the interview, focus on the present and the question being asked. Listen carefully, take time to think before answering, and avoid worrying about subsequent questions or future outcomes. By concentrating on the present moment, you'll feel more at ease and more involved in the interview.

7. Accept imperfection: Remember that nobody is perfect and recruiters don't expect you to answer every question perfectly. Accept that you may make mistakes or have blank moments. Remain calm and react confidently when this happens. Recruiters often appreciate the ability to handle the unexpected in a professional manner.

8. Learn from every interview: Every interview is a learning opportunity, whatever the outcome. After the interview, take time to reflect on your performance, what worked and what could be improved. Use this information to prepare yourself even better for future interviews. Each experience will make you more confident and better at managing stress and anxiety.

By managing stress and anxiety during the interview, you'll be able to present yourself more confidently and give your best. Proper preparation, relaxation techniques, a positive mindset and attention to your body language will help you overcome stress and feel more at ease during job interviews.

CHAPTER 8: MASTERING BEHAVIORAL INTERVIEWING TECHNIQUES

Behavioral interviews are becoming increasingly common in selection processes. These interviews focus on a candidate's past behaviors to predict future behavior in similar situations. Mastering behavioral interviewing techniques can help you answer competency- and behavior-based questions accurately and convincingly. In this chapter, we'll look at the principles of behavioral interviewing and give you tips on how to approach it successfully.

1. Understanding the STAR method: The STAR method (Situation, Task, Action, Result) is commonly used in behavioral interviewing. It helps you structure your answers by providing concrete examples of past behavior. The situation describes the context, the task represents the challenge or objective, the action describes the steps taken and the result outlines the results obtained.

2. Prepare concrete examples: Before the interview, identify concrete examples of past behavior that highlight your skills and experience. Review your career path and identify situations where you have demonstrated leadership, problem-solving, teamwork or other relevant skills. Prepare to describe these examples using the STAR method.

3. Be specific: When answering behavioral questions, be specific in your responses. Give concrete details of situations, actions taken and results achieved. Avoid vague or generalized answers. The more specific you are, the more convincing recruiters will find you.

4. Highlight your key skills: Behavioral interviews are an opportunity to highlight your key skills. Identify the skills that are most important for the position and prepare examples that demonstrate your mastery of these skills. Highlight your achievements, the challenges you've faced and how you've used your skills to overcome them.

5. Use measurable results: When describing the results of your actions, use quantifiable data whenever possible. For example, mention sales figures, cost savings, performance improvements or customer satisfaction rates. Measurable results reinforce your credibility and demonstrate the impact of your actions.

6. Stay focused on positive behaviors: When answering the behavioral questions, focus on the positive behaviors you have adopted. Emphasize your ability to solve problems, work as part of a team, take initiative and handle difficult situations constructively. Avoid talking about negative behaviors or situations in which you have failed.

7. Practice your answers: Practice your answers to behavioral questions using the STAR method. Practice describing situations, identifying the tasks you've performed, explaining the actions you've taken and detailing the results you've achieved. The more you practice, the more comfortable you'll feel in the interview.

8. Be ready to explain lessons learned: When you share your behavioral examples, be ready to explain the lessons you've learned from these experiences. Talk about the adjustments you made, the skills you developed or the strategies you put in place to improve results. Recruiters appreciate candidates who can reflect on their experiences and learn from them.

Behavioral interviews can be a challenge, but by understanding the basics and preparing properly, you'll be able to answer questions accurately and convincingly. Use the STAR method, prepare concrete examples and highlight your key skills. With practice and confidence, you can master behavioral interviewing and demonstrate your value to recruiters.

CHAPTER 9: USING BODY LANGUAGE TO YOUR ADVANTAGE

During a job interview, your body language plays a crucial role in how you are perceived by recruiters. Your posture, gestures, facial expression and eye contact can all influence how your message is received. In this chapter, we'll explore the importance of body language in a job interview and give you tips on how to use it to your advantage.

1. Maintain a confident posture: Your posture is a key element of your body language. Maintain an upright, open posture to show your confidence. Avoid slouching or crossing your arms, as this can give the impression that you're closed or unsure of yourself. A confident posture conveys a positive image and reinforces your presence at the interview.

2. Make eye contact: Eye contact is an essential component of communication. When talking to recruiters, maintain regular eye contact to show your commitment and interest. Avoid constantly looking away or looking down, as this can give the impression that you lack confidence. Be careful not to maintain too much eye contact, as this can be perceived as aggressive.

3. Smile naturally: A warm smile can create a positive impression during an interview. Smile naturally and appropriately throughout the interview, especially when introducing yourself or sharing positive information. A smile conveys a positive attitude and openness to conversation.

4. Use appropriate gestures: Gestures can enhance your communication, but it's important to use them appropriately. Use natural, measured gestures to accompany your words and emphasize important points. Avoid excessive, agitated or repetitive gestures, as these can distract recruiters. Be aware of your body language and use it to support what you say.

5. Avoid nervous movements: During the interview, watch out for nervous movements such as playing with a pen, tapping your fingers or shaking your leg. These movements can give the impression that you're anxious or distracted. Try to remain calm and controlled, keeping your movements under control.

6. Be receptive to recruiters' non-verbal cues: In addition to mastering your own body language, pay attention to recruiters' non-verbal cues. Observe their body language for signs of interest, concern or disagreement. Adapt your communication accordingly to respond to their signals and establish a better connection.

7. Adapt your body language to the company's culture: Every company has its own culture and body language standards. Research the company to understand its communication style and adapt your body language accordingly. For example, some companies may value a more relaxed and informal body language, while others may expect a more formal approach.

8. Practice your body language: To use body language to your advantage, practice in front of a mirror or with a friend. Observe your expressions, gestures and posture, and adjust them if necessary. Do mock interviews to get used to using your body language effectively and naturally.

Your body language can reinforce your message and convey a positive image during a job interview. By maintaining a confident posture, making eye contact, smiling naturally and using appropriate gestures, you can establish a stronger connection with recruiters. Practice your body language and adapt it to the company's culture to maximize your impact during interviews.

CHAPTER 10: NEGOTIATING SALARY AND BENEFITS

Negotiating salary and benefits is an important step in the hiring process. It's essential to demonstrate your value and skills in order to obtain compensation and benefits that match your expectations. In this chapter, we'll look at the importance of negotiating salary and benefits, and give you tips on how to conduct a successful negotiation.

1. Do your research: Before entering into any salary negotiations, thoroughly research the salaries and benefits offered for similar positions in your industry and region. Consult reliable sources such as job boards, salary reports and professional associations. Having accurate data will give you a solid basis for your negotiation.

2. Know your value: Evaluate your skills, experience and achievements to determine your value on the job market. Think about what you bring to the company in terms of knowledge, skills and results. The more you know about your value, the more you'll be able to justify your demands during negotiations.

3. Set your goals: Before negotiating, determine your goals in terms of salary and benefits. Define a realistic salary range based on your research and skills. Also identify the benefits that are important to you, such as work flexibility, fringe benefits or training and development opportunities. Having a clear vision of your objectives will help you feel confident and prepared when negotiating.

4. Choose the right moment: Select the right moment to begin salary negotiations. Ideally, wait until the employer has expressed an interest in you and made you an offer. This will give you a better negotiating position. Be prepared to discuss your compensation and benefits at this stage, highlighting your qualifications and presenting solid arguments.

5. Prepare your arguments: Before the negotiation, prepare your arguments to justify your salary and benefits requests. Highlight your skills, your achievements and the benefits you will bring to the company. Use concrete examples to illustrate your added value. Also prepare answers to any objections the employer may raise.

6. Start by asking for more: When you start negotiating, start by asking for a slightly higher salary than your actual target. This will give you leeway in the negotiations and enable you to obtain a salary closer to your expectations. Be confident and present your arguments clearly and convincingly.

7. Be flexible: Salary negotiations often involve a certain amount of compromise. Be prepared to be flexible and find solutions that work for both you and the employer. For example, if the company can't increase your salary, you can negotiate additional benefits such as extra days off, professional training or opportunities for

advancement.

8. Listen carefully: When negotiating, listen carefully to the employer's arguments and proposals. Be open to discussion and show interest in the company's needs. Understand that negotiation is a process of exchange and the search for mutually beneficial solutions.

9. Be ready to make a decision: When you reach agreement on salary and benefits, be ready to make a decision. Weigh the pros and cons of the offer, taking into account your goals and personal situation. If the offer doesn't meet your expectations, be prepared to politely decline and look for other opportunities.

Negotiating salary and benefits is an important step in establishing fair compensation and obtaining benefits that match your expectations. Do thorough research, know your value, set your goals and prepare your arguments. Be flexible, listen carefully and be prepared to make an informed decision. Successful negotiation can help you obtain compensation and benefits that reflect your professional value.

CHAPTER 11: AVOIDING COMMON INTERVIEW MISTAKES

During a job interview, it's natural to want to make the best possible impression on recruiters. However, it's important to recognize and avoid common mistakes that could jeopardize your chances of getting the job. In this chapter, we'll look at the most common interview mistakes and give you tips on how to avoid them.

1. Arriving late: One of the most common mistakes is arriving late for an interview. It gives an impression of disorganization and disrespect towards recruiters. Make sure you plan your journey in advance, allow for any delays and arrive early enough to settle in and get ready.

2. Lack of preparation: Not preparing sufficiently for an interview is a major mistake. Thoroughly research the company, the position and the people you'll be interviewing with. Prepare answers to common questions, and prepare concrete examples of your skills and achievements. Being well prepared will enable you to answer more convincingly and show your interest in the position.

3. Lack of confidence: Lack of confidence can manifest itself in hesitant body language, a weak tone of voice or vague answers. It's important to believe in your skills and your worth. Practice your answers in advance, use relaxation techniques to calm your nerves and remind yourself of past achievements. A confident attitude will reinforce your image with recruiters.

4. Responding inappropriately: It's crucial to respond appropriately to interview questions. Avoid answers that are too long or too short, stay focused on the question and answer clearly and concisely. Listen carefully to questions and take time to think before answering. Be aware of your body language as you answer, and show commitment and interest.

5. Don't ask questions: At the end of the interview, recruiters usually give you the opportunity to ask your own questions. Not asking questions can give the impression that you're not interested in the position or the company. Prepare a list of relevant questions about the company, the position, the corporate culture or development opportunities. This will demonstrate your interest and commitment to the company.

6. Criticize former employers: Avoid criticizing your former employers during the interview, even if you've had negative experiences. Remain professional and focused on the lessons learned and skills acquired through these experiences. Recruiters appreciate candidates who can handle difficult situations constructively and positively.

7. Lack of follow-up: After the interview, it's essential to follow up with the recruiters to thank the recruiting team and reaffirm your interest in the position. Neglecting to follow up can give the impression that you're not sufficiently motivated or interested.

Send a thank-you e-mail within 24 to 48 hours of the interview to maintain a good impression.

8. Not being authentic: It's important to be yourself at the interview. Trying to be someone else or answering artificially can be easily detected by recruiters. Be honest, transparent and authentic in your answers. Show your true personality while remaining professional.

Avoiding these common interview mistakes can improve your chances of success. Make sure you arrive on time, prepare accordingly and demonstrate your confidence. Respond appropriately, ask relevant questions and avoid negative criticism. Follow up after the interview and be authentic. By avoiding these mistakes, you'll be able to present yourself in the best possible light and stand out from the crowd.

CHAPTER 12: SETTING YOURSELF APART FROM OTHER CANDIDATES

In a competitive job market, standing out from the crowd can make all the difference in the selection process. Recruiters are looking for candidates who stand out from the crowd, add value and demonstrate motivation and commitment. In this chapter, we'll explore different strategies for setting yourself apart from other candidates and increasing your chances of success.

1. Make a memorable first impression: The first impression you make on recruiters is crucial. Be professional, polite and well-prepared from the first moment of contact. Dress appropriately, maintain confident body language and be courteous to all members of the recruitment team. A positive first impression will immediately set you apart from other candidates.

2. Personalize your application: Don't just send a generic application. Personalize your CV, cover letter and other documentation to show that you've taken the time to understand the company and the position. Highlight your relevant skills and

achievements that match the company's needs. A personalized application demonstrates your genuine interest and investment in the opportunity.

3. Highlight your achievements: When describing your past experiences, emphasize your accomplishments and the results you've achieved. Recruiters are interested in what you've accomplished and how you can contribute to their company. Use figures, statistics or concrete examples to illustrate your achievements. This will help you stand out from other candidates.

4. Show your motivation: Recruiters are looking for motivated and passionate candidates. Express your interest in the company, the position and the industry during the interview. Talk about why you're attracted to this specific opportunity and how you can contribute to achieving the company's goals. Genuine motivation can set you apart from other candidates who may seem less committed.

5. Highlight your unique skills: Identify your unique and differentiating skills and highlight them at interview. Whether it's a particular technical skill, international experience or leadership talents, make sure recruiters recognize what sets you apart from other candidates. Highlight how these skills can add value to the company.

6. Be ready to share innovative ideas: During the interview, prepare innovative ideas that are relevant to the company. Show that you've taken the time to familiarize yourself with the challenges facing the company, and come up with creative solutions. This will demonstrate your strategic thinking and your ability to bring new perspectives to the table.

7. Develop your professional network: Invest in developing your professional network. Attend events, conferences or webinars related to your field of activity. Connect with influential professionals in your industry and maintain strong professional relationships. An extensive network can give you access to unique opportunities and help you stand out from other candidates.

8. Continue to learn and develop: Demonstrate your willingness to learn and develop continuously. Mention any training, certifications or learning initiatives you've undertaken to strengthen your skills. Recruiters appreciate candidates who are willing to improve and stay up to date in their field.

9. Be authentic: Finally, be yourself. Show your true personality and let your values and work ethic shine through. Recruiters are looking to connect with candidates and find those who fit the company culture. Be authentic and let your personality shine through.

By putting these strategies into practice, you can set yourself apart from other candidates and attract the attention of recruiters. Make a memorable first impression, personalize your application, highlight your achievements and motivation, and demonstrate your unique skills. Keep learning, develop your professional network and remain authentic throughout the selection process. By setting yourself apart from other candidates, you increase your chances of success and getting the job you want.

CHAPTER 13: USING SOCIAL NETWORKS TO FIND A JOB

In today's world, social networks play an increasingly important role in the job search. Platforms such as LinkedIn, Twitter and Facebook offer unique opportunities to connect with professionals, search for job vacancies and promote your personal brand. In this chapter, we'll explore how to effectively use social networks to optimize your job search.

1. Create a professional profile: The first step to using social networks in your job search is to create a solid professional profile. On LinkedIn, update your profile with a captivating summary, a professional photo and a comprehensive list of your skills, experience and achievements. Make sure, too, that your other social networking profiles reflect an appropriate, professional image.

2. Expand your network: Social networks offer a unique opportunity to connect with professionals in your field. Look for influencers, recruiters or professionals who work in the companies that interest you. Send them a personalized connection request, explaining your common interest and your willingness to learn more. Expanding your network will give you

access to new opportunities, advice and recommendations.

3. Share relevant content: Use social networks to share relevant content related to your area of expertise. Publish articles, videos or links to interesting resources. Share your thoughts and ideas on relevant topics. This will demonstrate your expertise and interest in your field, attracting the attention of recruiters and potential employers.

4. Search for job offers: Social networks are full of job opportunities. Follow company pages, professional groups and accounts dedicated to employment. Pay close attention to job postings and use search tools to find opportunities that match your skills and interests. Don't hesitate to apply online or contact recruiters directly.

5. Interact with potential employers: Social networks offer the opportunity to interact directly with potential employers. Comment on the publications of companies that interest you, ask questions or take part in relevant discussions. Show your interest and commitment to the company. This interaction can help you get noticed and build relationships with key decision-makers.

6. Take care of your e-reputation: When using social networks in your job search, it's important to take care of your e-reputation. Make sure your posts, comments and interactions reflect a positive, professional image. Avoid controversial or inappropriate posts that could damage your candidacy. Recruiters can view your profile online, so make sure that what they find reinforces your professional image.

7. Take advantage of the specific features of each social network: Each social network offers specific features that you can use to

optimize your job search. On LinkedIn, for example, you can ask for recommendations, join professional groups or use the job search tool. Explore these features and take advantage of them to maximize your chances of success.

8. Stay active and engaged: To take full advantage of social networks in your job search, stay active and engage regularly. Share updates, comment on others' posts and reply to messages. The more active and engaged you are, the more visible you'll be to recruiters and potential employers.

By using social networks effectively, you can expand your professional network, search for job opportunities, share your expertise and interact with potential employers. Create a solid professional profile, share relevant content, search for job offers and actively interact with professionals in your field. By using social networks strategically, you can increase your chances of finding job opportunities and standing out from other candidates.

CHAPTER 14: PROFESSIONAL FOLLOW-UP AFTER THE INTERVIEW

After an interview, a professional follow-up is essential to strengthen your candidacy and maintain a good relationship with recruiters. Professional follow-up demonstrates your interest and commitment to the position, while keeping you top of mind with recruiters. In this chapter, we'll explore the importance of professional follow-up and give you tips on how to do it effectively.

1. Send a thank-you e-mail: Within 24 to 48 hours of the interview, send a thank-you e-mail to the people you interacted with. Address each person individually and express your gratitude for their time. Mention specific points from the interview that particularly interested or impressed you. Show your enthusiasm for the position and your interest in continuing the selection process.

2. Be concise and professional: When writing your thank-you e-mail, be concise and professional. Avoid messages that are too

long or too informal. Be sure to proofread and correct any spelling or grammatical errors before sending the e-mail. Use a polite and respectful tone while remaining authentic in your expression of gratitude.

3. Recap interview highlights: Take advantage of the thank-you e-mail to briefly recall some of the interview highlights. Mention specific skills, experience or achievements that were discussed. This reinforces your application and shows that you have retained the key information from the interview.

4. Tailor your message to each person: If you've had exchanges with several people, tailor your message to each person. Refer to specific discussion points you've had with each individual. This demonstrates your attention to detail and personal consideration for each member of the recruitment team.

5. Stay professional on social networks: After the interview, continue to be professional on social networks. Avoid inappropriate or controversial posts that could compromise your professional image. Recruiters can view your profile online, so make sure that what they find reinforces your candidacy and presents a positive image of you.

6. Follow agreed deadlines: If recruiters have given you an estimate of when they will make a decision, follow the agreed deadlines. Don't send repetitive e-mails or excessive reminders. Respect the selection process and wait patiently for their reply.

7. Follow up appropriately: If it's been a while since you've heard back, it's okay to follow up appropriately. Send a polite e-mail asking about the status of your application. Briefly remind them of your interest in the position and ask if they need any more

information from you. Bear in mind that selection times can vary depending on various factors, so be patient and respectful in your approach.

8. Remain positive and professional in the event of rejection: If you receive a negative reply, remain positive and professional in your response. Express your gratitude for the opportunity to have participated in the selection process and thank them for considering you for the position. Ask if you can keep in touch for possible future opportunities. Keeping a positive and professional attitude, even in the event of rejection, can open doors to future contacts or professional opportunities.

Professional follow-up after the interview is an important step in strengthening your application and maintaining a good relationship with recruiters. Send a timely thank-you email, personalizing your message, recalling the highlights of the interview. Be professional on social networks, respect agreed deadlines and make appropriate follow-ups if necessary. Maintain a positive and professional attitude, even in the event of rejection. Professional follow-up shows your professionalism and interest in the position, which can set you apart from other candidates and open doors to future opportunities.

CHAPTER 15: SUCCESSFUL TELEPHONE AND ONLINE INTERVIEWS

With the evolution of technology and the new realities of the working world, telephone and online interviews have become commonplace steps in the selection process. These types of interviews offer flexibility for both recruiters and candidates, but they also present particular challenges. In this chapter, we explore strategies and best practices for successful telephone and online interviews.

1. Prepare as you would for a face-to-face interview: Even if the interview takes place remotely, it's important to prepare as you would for a face-to-face interview. Learn about the company and the position, prepare answers to common questions and practice your presentation. Also make sure you have a stable Internet connection, a quiet environment and the right equipment, such as headphones and a working webcam.

2. Test your equipment: Before servicing, test your equipment to make sure it's working properly. Check the audio and video

quality of your microphone, speakers and webcam. Also make sure you have the latest version of the software required for online maintenance, whether Zoom, Skype or similar platforms. By carrying out these preliminary tests, you'll avoid technical problems during the interview.

3. Create a conducive environment: Choose a quiet, well-lit location for your interview. Eliminate potential distractions, such as background noise or unexpected interruptions. Provide a clean, professional space in the background. Also make sure you have a reliable Internet connection to avoid interruptions during the interview.

4. Dress professionally: Even if you're at home, dress professionally for the interview. Choose clothes that are appropriate for the company and the position, as if you were going to an interview in person. This will help put you in the right frame of mind and show your commitment to the interview.

5. Pay attention to your body language: Even if recruiters can only partially see you during a telephone or online interview, your body language still plays an important role. Sit up straight, maintain eye contact with the camera and show commitment and enthusiasm in your voice. Smile and use appropriate gestures to reinforce your message. Your body language will convey a professional and positive image to recruiters.

6. Speak clearly and listen carefully: During the interview, speak clearly and avoid speaking too quickly. Be aware of your voice and diction. Listen carefully to recruiters' questions and take time to think before answering. Be patient and polite in online interactions.

7. Use reminder notes: One of the advantages of telephone and online interviews is that you can use reminder notes. Prepare key points, examples or questions you want to address and keep them handy. However, be careful not to rely too heavily on your notes and maintain eye contact with recruiters as much as possible.

8. Follow the same rules of professional follow-up: After the telephone or online interview, send a thank-you e-mail to express your gratitude and reaffirm your interest in the position. Follow the same rules of professional follow-up as for a face-to-face interview.

Telephone and online interviews present unique challenges, but by preparing properly and following best practices, you can succeed. Prepare as you would for a face-to-face interview, test your equipment, create a conducive environment and dress professionally. Be aware of your body language, speak clearly and listen carefully. Use reminder notes judiciously and follow the same rules of professional follow-up. By following these tips, you'll be well equipped to succeed in telephone and online interviews and stand out from the crowd.

CONCLUSION: ACHIEVING SUCCESS IN A JOB INTERVIEW

In this book, we have explored in detail the different stages and key aspects of a successful job interview. We've covered preparation, the importance of researching the company and the job in advance, how to highlight your skills and experience, and techniques for standing out from other candidates.

We also discussed the importance of self-confidence, effective communication, stress and anxiety management, as well as the use of social networks and online interviews. All these steps are essential to maximize your chances of success at a job interview.

It's crucial to understand that every interview is an opportunity to present yourself authentically and professionally. Every interaction with recruiters is an opportunity to demonstrate your value, expertise and motivation for the job. Every question asked is an opportunity to demonstrate your ability to solve problems, work in a team and adapt to professional situations.

Preparation is the key to a successful job interview. By investing time and effort in research, preparing answers to common questions, and identifying and emphasizing your strengths, you give yourself the best chance of success.

However, it's important to remember that, despite careful preparation, there may be times when you feel less confident, or when you get an answer wrong. In these situations, it's important to stay calm, refocus and continue to give your best. Recruiters value authenticity and the ability to face challenges with professionalism.

After the interview, it's essential to follow up professionally, whether with a thank-you email or appropriate follow-ups. This shows your commitment and interest in the position, and maintains a good relationship with the recruiters.

In conclusion, a successful job interview requires a combination of preparation, self-confidence, communication skills and adaptability. It's a process that's constantly evolving, taking into account new technologies and the new realities of the working world.

This book aims to provide you with the tools and knowledge you need to approach a job interview with confidence and success. Keep in mind that every experience is an opportunity for learning and professional growth.

We encourage you to continue preparing, developing your skills and maintaining a positive attitude throughout your career. With the right preparation, the right self-confidence and the will to improve, you'll be able to succeed in job interviews and get closer to your career goals.

We wish you all the best in your future professional opportunities, and hope this book has helped you on your way to job interview success.

Good luck!

* 9 7 9 8 3 9 6 1 3 2 1 5 3 *